I Am the Jackpot

This book is a work of inspiration and empowerment. The content herein is intended for informational and motivational purposes only. It does not guarantee lottery winnings, financial results, or specific outcomes. Readers are responsible for their own choices and are encouraged to play responsibly and seek professional financial, legal, or medical counsel where appropriate. The author and publisher disclaim any liability arising directly or indirectly from the use or application of the material in this book.

Published by: My Littl' Workshop (MLW)
U.S.A.

Cover & Interior Design: MLW Studios
Printed in the United States of America

Dedication

I dedicate this book to myself, for daring to believe I am the jackpot.

To my ancestors, who aligned my steps before I could see the path.

And to every reader bold enough to claim their own win – may you remember that the true jackpot is already within you.

Acknowledgments

First, I honor myself – for daring to believe, for writing these words, and for standing in alignment with abundance even when the world tried to silence me.

I honor my ancestors, known and unknown, who walked before me, cleared paths, and whispered wisdom into my bones. Every prayer, every sacrifice, every tear they shed is carried in my victories. This book is not mine alone—it belongs to them too.

I acknowledge the Divine Source who makes all things possible, who reminds me daily that abundance is my natural state and that no weapon formed against me shall ever prosper.

And I thank you, the reader – for having the courage to pick up this book, to believe in yourself, and to declare that you too are the jackpot. May these words empower you, protect you, and remind you that your wealth, health, and legacy are already here.

So it is, and so it will forever be.

Disclaimer

This book is written for inspiration, motivation, and spiritual alignment only. It does not guarantee lottery winnings or financial outcomes. The affirmations, declarations, and practices within are tools for mindset, energy work, and personal empowerment.

Readers are encouraged to play responsibly, never gamble what they cannot afford to lose, and seek professional advice (legal, financial, medical, or otherwise) before making major decisions. The author is not liable for any personal choices, risks, or outcomes resulting from the use of this material.

Remember: wealth begins in the mind, in health, and in spirit. Align wisely.

"Before You Begin"

You are not chasing millions. Millions are chasing you. You are not trying to win. You are the win. You are the jackpot.

This book is your reminder that the real fortune begins in the mind, the tongue, and the spirit. Inside you'll find affirmations, declarations, mantras, vows, prayers, and practices to align you with abundance, protect your energy, and prepare you to live richly and responsibly.

When it is your moment, nothing and no one can block you. Until then, live as if it is already done — because in truth, it is.

I Am the Jackpot

The Vow: I Am the Jackpot

"I am the jackpot.
I am the blessing.
I am the abundance walking toward my destiny.
Every day, I grow closer to my win.
Every day, I align deeper with my millions.
Whether it is 5,000, 5 million, 5 billion, or more—
there are no limits to what I may receive.
I wait with patience.
I receive under grace and in perfect timing.
My jackpot is certain, my overflow is guaranteed.
I vow to enjoy it fully,
to savor every blessing,
to celebrate every bit of what comes to me.
No barrier is strong enough to block me.
No wall is high enough to stop me.
No delay can deny me.
My progress and productivity flow without
resistance.

I am the jackpot.
I am the chosen.

I am aligned with victory, prosperity, and legacy.
So it is, so it must be, so it already is."

Author's Note on Repetition

As you read this book, you may notice that some ideas – especially in Chapter 7 and in other key places – appear more than once. This is not by accident. Repetition is one of the most powerful tools to reprogram the subconscious mind.

When you hear something once, it may inspire you. When you hear it again, it begins to take root. And when you repeat it enough times, it becomes a part of you – an unshakable truth.

So yes, certain affirmations, practices, and warnings are repeated in these pages. They are imperative. They are meant to reach deeper into you until your cells, your spirit, and your subconscious all respond with, "I know this. I live this. This is who I am."

Do not skip over repetition. Embrace it. Every time you meet it again, let it sink further into your mind and spirit. Because sometimes, hearing it the second or third time is when it finally becomes real for you.

A Letter to the Winner

Beloved Winner,

If you are holding this book in your hands, know this: the universe already calls you chosen. You did not arrive here by accident. Every page you read will remind you of who you already are – the jackpot, the abundance, the blessing.

May you never again wait for permission to shine. May you never again give your power away to strangers, fear, or desperation.
May you rise daily with gratitude, with clarity, with protection.

Be patient with yourself, and trust the timing of you life. When it is your moment, nothing and no one ca block you. Until then, live as if it is already done because in truth, it is.

Remember: wealth is not only in numbers. It is in y spirit, your health, your love, your legacy. Walk ric speak richly, live richly. Protect your peace fierc and honor those who came before you.

I leave you with this truth: You are not cha millions. Millions are chasing you. You are not tr to win. You are the win. You are the jackpot.

So it is, and so it will forever be.

With strength, clarity, and love,
Rev. Dr. Marie Brevil

Table of Contents

- Sample Winner's List (example)
- Journal prompts to build your list
- Mini ritual: Writing your Winner's List
- Affirmations & Declaration of Readiness

The Winner's List May Include:

1. Legal & Financial Protection:
    - Hire a lawyer who understands high net worth management.
    - Hire a financial advisor and accountant.
    - Decide which bank (FDIC insured; consider limits and multiple accounts).
    - Create an estate plan, trust, or LLC.
    - Set up trust funds for nieces, nephews, siblings.
2. Living & Lifestyle:
    - Where will you live? (new house, gated community, country estate).
    - Upgrade wardrobe, car, and security.
    - Hire an assistant or personal staff.
3. Health & Wellbeing:
    - Fix teeth, see dermatologist, nutritionist.
    - Invest in holistic and medical care.
    - Fitness, yoga, meditation coaches.
4. Family & Legacy:
    - Take care of parents, siblings.
    - Pay for education (self or children).
    - Honor ancestors with land, libations, memorials.
5. Contribution & Expansion:
    - Invest in businesses.
    - Support charities.
    - Create community programs.
    - Fund spiritual or cultural legacies.

Chapter 4 — The First 72 Hours After Winning

- What to do immediately when you know you've won
- Stay quiet, breathe, don't tell everyone
- Secure your ticket, sign it, and store it safely
- Spiritual grounding: prayer, libation, gratitude
- Decide who you can truly trust
- Safety in celebration
- Lessons from sad stories of past winners
- The Sacred Vow of Self-Priority
- 7 Mantras of Protection & Self-Priority
- Affirmations & Declaration of Calm Victory

Chapter 5 — Maintaining Wealth, Not Returning to Poverty

- The millionaire mindset vs. the poverty mindset
- Master Manifestor language: no more "I need" — only "I have"
- How to invest and grow wealth
- Schools, businesses, spiritual investments
- Spiritual, personal, and social guidance (spiritual leaders, coaches, etiquette training)
- Mistakes that drain wealth
- How to live richly and responsibly
- Affirmations & Declaration of Permanent Abundance

Chapter 6 — Affirmations for Winners Only

- Lotto affirmations (I already have the millions)
- Jackpot declarations
- Abundance affirmations for everyday wealth
- Health, love, and legacy affirmations

Play to Win, But Play Responsibly

Playing the lottery is not about chasing luck—it's about stepping into alignment with possibility. But with that, there must be discipline. You are not here to gamble recklessly; you are here to command your reality.

Playing responsibly means knowing when, how, and why you play.

The Real Jackpot Starts in the Mind

Before the numbers are drawn, before the ticket is printed, before the prize is claimed—the true jackpot is your mindset. The richest treasure is already within you. If you think poor, you will remain poor even if millions fall into your hands. If you think rich, your wealth multiplies no matter where it comes from.

Aligning Energy Before Aligning Numbers

Numbers are just symbols; energy is what gives them life. You cannot win consistently with a scattered, desperate, or fearful spirit. When your vibration is calm, abundant, and aligned, the right opportunities and outcomes appear. You don't chase numbers; you align with the frequency that attracts them.

Why Affirmations Work

Affirmations are not magic words; they are energy codes. When spoken with belief, they reprogram your subconscious shift your frequency, and bend reality to match your vibration. The law of attraction, the law of abundance, and the law of certainty work together:

- You attract what you believe.
- You multiply what you affirm.
- You receive what you claim with certainty.

This book is about learning to play from a place of power —not lack—and to speak your winnings into existence before they arrive.

Let's begin with some powerful affirmations.

Let's begin with a powerful starting set of affirmations crafted specifically for winning the lotto (Mega Millions, Powerball, and other big draws). These affirmations are very bold, rhythmic, and energetically charged, so if you speak them with conviction, like a prayer and a declaration combined.

Lotto & Jackpot Affirmations

- I am aligned with the frequency of abundance, wealth flows to me now effortlessly.
- Mega Millions is mine, Powerball is mine, the jackpot belongs to me irrevocably.
- Every number I choose aligns with divine favor and prosperity.
- Money is energy, and I command it to come to me in overflowing amounts under grace and perfect way.
- I am a magnet for jackpot blessings, miracles, and unexpected riches.
- I see myself holding the winning ticket, and so it is.
- Fortune favors me always—I win every time, in every game.
- I play with certainty, and certainty brings me victory.
- The universe selects me as the winner because I am ready and worthy.
- I claim my millions now—I am the rightful owner of unlimited wealth.

General Game-Winning Affirmations

- I win every game I play because I vibrate with victory.
- Favor follows me, luck serves me, destiny chooses me.
- My spirit, my hands, my choices are guided toward triumph.
- The winning outcome is always mine—I was born to succeed.
- Every roll, every draw, every card bends to my favor.
- I attract winning streaks like the sun attracts the dawn.
- I am unstoppable, unshakable, unbreakable—I win always.
- Every time I play, I multiply my wealth and blessings.
- Victory is my birthright, and I claim it now.
- I am chosen for greatness, and my wins prove it.

7 Daily Lotto Affirmations

Speak one each day or all seven together before buying/holding your ticket:

1. I am aligned with the jackpot—I claim my millions today.
2. My numbers are chosen in divine perfection; I am the winner.
3. Mega Millions, Powerball, and all games bend to my favor.
4. I hold the winning ticket with gratitude and joy.
5. Wealth rushes into my life easily and abundantly.
6. My hands are blessed, my spirit is favored, my ticket is golden.
7. Today, I am the multi-millionaire the universe has chosen.

7 Daily Game-Winning Affirmations

Use these when playing any game, small or big:

- Victory is my nature; I win every time I play.
- Every game surrenders its prize to me with ease.
- I am luck, I am fortune, I am destiny fulfilled.
- My energy is aligned with success—I cannot lose.
- Triumph flows through me; I attract winning streaks.
- Favor follows me wherever I play, whatever I touch.
- Winning is mine because I command it into being.

7 Jackpot Declarations (Powerful Incantations)

These are longer, like spoken spells—say them with power and visualization:

1. "I stand as the chosen vessel of abundance; this jackpot is mine, secured, sealed, and delivered."
2. "Every draw bends toward my destiny; every number calls my name."
3. "I am already the winner—my millions are here, and I rejoice in receiving them now."
4. "By divine favor, by universal law, I command wealth, I command victory, I command fortune."
5. "Luck, chance, and fate bow to me—I am the victorious one."
6. "I hold the ticket of destiny, and it overflows with riches beyond measure."
7. "So it is, so it shall be—I am a jackpot winner, chosen and crowned."

Chapter 1 – Responsible Play, Responsible Power

Chapter 1 — Responsible Play, Responsible Power

The First Rule: Respect the Power of Money and Chance

Money is not evil, but it magnifies whatever energy is already present in your life. If you are careless, money amplifies recklessness. If you are wise, money amplifies wisdom. Winning the lottery or any jackpot is not just about holding a lucky ticket—it's about holding power. And with power comes responsibility.

That is why before we even talk about affirmations, visualization, and manifesting, we must talk about responsible play.

To play responsibly is to know that your life, your family, your health, and your purpose must never be sacrificed for a ticket. It means you never put the grocery money, the rent money, or your child's meal into a lotto slip. Lotto should never be played out of desperation, fear, or lack. That vibration only multiplies the same energy.

Responsible play is not poverty thinking—it is powerful thinking. It says:

"I play because I align with abundance, not because I am running from lack."

What Responsible Play Looks Like

- If you cannot visualize yourself winning, wait until you can. Your mindset is your true ticket.

- If you must choose between playing and feeding your child, always feed your child. You cannot manifest abundance from neglect.
- If you feel anxious, desperate, or hopeless while playing, stop and reset. Only play when your spirit is aligned.
- Set a limit. Maybe it's $10 a week, maybe less, maybe none at all. Never more than you are willing to walk away from with peace.

The Real Jackpot is Alignment

Playing the lottery is symbolic. You are stepping into a stream of possibility, but your true power is in your alignment with abundance. If your spirit is saying "I already won," you will always be wealthy—whether through lotto, business, investments, or unexpected blessings.

You are not a beggar. You are not chasing. You are aligning.

And when you align, you become the winner long before the numbers are drawn.

Affirmations for Responsible Play

Speak these before every ticket, before every game, before every decision:

- I am aligned with abundance, not desperation.
- I play with joy, wisdom, and clarity.
- I never chase money; I attract it with ease.
- I am responsible with my power, my money, and my destiny.
- I honor my family, my body, and my spirit before I play.
- I see the lotto not as a savior but as a blessing aligned with my path.
- I win in life because I am already wealthy within.

Reflective Journal Prompt

- What does responsible play mean to me personally?
- Have I ever played from desperation instead of alignment? How did that feel?
- What boundaries can I set so I play only with wisdom and peace?

Declaration of Responsible Power

Repeat this like a sacred vow:

"I am a master of my choices. I play only when my spirit is aligned, when my life is in balance, and when my heart is full. I will never neglect what is sacred for a chance at fortune. I am responsible, I am powerful, and abundance flows to me naturally. My play is guided, my money is safe, and my life is always cared for."

What it Means to Play Responsibly

Playing responsibly means your bills are paid, your children are fed, your home is stable, and your health is cared for before you spend a single dollar on lotto. A ticket should never come at the cost of your necessities. If you cannot afford to lose it, you cannot afford to play it.

- Do not starve your children to play.
- Do not gamble away the rent or mortgage.
- Do not risk your peace of mind on desperation.

Lotto should feel like an overflow, never a burden.

Playing with Alignment, Not Desperation

There are two ways people play:

- From lack: "I need this win or else…"
- From abundance: "I play because I am already abundant, and this is just one of many ways my wealth may arrive."

One brings anxiety, the other brings flow. Desperation pushes blessings away; alignment magnetizes them.

The Energy of "I Am" vs. "I Want"

The words you use reveal your vibration.

- "I want" is a beggar's cry. It says you do not have, and so the universe keeps you wanting.
- "I am" is a master's declaration. It says you already hold it, and so the universe delivers to match your certainty.

The Energy of "I Am" vs. "I Want" (Repeat)

The words you use reveal your vibration.

- "I want" is a beggar's cry. It says you do not have, and so the universe keeps you wanting.
- "I am" is a master's declaration. It says you already hold it, and so the universe delivers to match your certainty.

Say "I am wealthy," not "I want money."
Say "I am the jackpot winner," not "I need to win."
Say "I am aligned with abundance," not "I hope I get lucky."

Winners do not hope—they know.

Affirmations for Responsible Power

- I honor my responsibilities before I play.
- I play only from overflow, never from lack.
- I align my energy with certainty, not desperation.
- I am the jackpot winner in spirit before I am in reality.
- I respect money, and money respects me.
- I choose wisely, I play wisely, and I receive wisely.
- I am always cared for, whether I play or not.

Declaration of Responsible Play

"I will never dishonor my life or my loved ones for the chance of riches. I am not desperate; I am aligned. I do not chase numbers—I attract abundance. I am powerful, responsible, and ready for wealth. The jackpot is mine because I am already rich within."

The Energy of "I Am" vs. "I Want"

The words you speak are contracts with the universe. When you say "I want", you confess lack. You create a vibration that keeps you always wanting, always reaching, but never receiving. Wanting is an admission of emptiness.

When you say "I am", you declare identity. You speak as if the blessing is already yours. And because the universe mirrors certainty, it responds by delivering what you have claimed.

The Energy of "I Have" vs. "I Need"

"Need" is the lowest vibration of all. When you say "I need money", you call forth struggle, survival, and desperation. The universe will only give you situations where you still need, never where you overflow.

But when you say "I have", you step into the reality of ownership. "I have the winning ticket. I have the millions. I have the abundance I asked for." Even if the paper is not yet in your hand, your energy is already in possession.

- Need cries.
- Have commands.
- Need is lack.
- Have is overflow.

Winners speak in I have, not I need.

Affirmations for "I Have" Energy

1. I have the winning numbers aligned to my destiny.
2. I have the abundance I desire—it is already mine.
3. I have overflow, wealth, and prosperity in every area of my life.
4. I have the jackpot blessing, sealed and secured.
5. I have all I require to live well, give well, and love well.
6. I have victory in my hands, my spirit, and my future.
7. I have it now, and nothing can stop it from manifesting.

Declaration of Having

"I no longer beg, chase, or cry for what is already mine. I do not say I need; I say I have. I have the millions, I have the victory, I have the abundance, I have the peace, I have the freedom. Because I have it in my mind, I have it in my life. So it is, and so it must be."

TO DO LIST

DATE: ____________________ DUE DATE ____________________

TO DO

- [ ] ____________________
- [ ] ____________________
- [ ] ____________________
- [ ] ____________________
- [ ] ____________________
- [ ] ____________________
- [ ] ____________________
- [ ] ____________________
- [ ] ____________________
- [ ] ____________________
- [ ] ____________________
- [ ] ____________________
- [ ] ____________________
- [ ] ____________________
- [ ] ____________________
- [ ] ____________________
- [ ] ____________________
- [ ] ____________________
- [ ] ____________________
- [ ] ____________________
- [ ] ____________________
- [ ] ____________________
- [ ] ____________________
- [ ] ____________________
- [ ] ____________________
- [ ] ____________________

PRIORITIES

- [ ] ____________________
- [ ] ____________________
- [ ] ____________________
- [ ] ____________________
- [ ] ____________________
- [ ] ____________________
- [ ] ____________________

NOTES

REMINDER

Notes

Chapter 2 – Visualization & Alignment

How to Visualize Holding the Winning Ticket

Close your eyes. See the numbers printed on the paper. Feel the ticket in your hands as if it is already stamped "Winner." Imagine the moment your heart jumps when the numbers are called. Picture the joy, the celebration, the calls you'll make, the prayers of gratitude you'll speak.

Visualization is not wishful thinking—it is energetic rehearsal. When you see it in your mind, you instruct the universe to match your vision.

Using Breathwork, Declarations, and Meditation Before Playing

- Breathwork: Inhale abundance, exhale lack. Breathe in slowly for 7 counts, hold for 4, exhale for 8. Each breath is you releasing fear and claiming certainty.
- Declarations: Speak out loud—"I am the jackpot winner. I am aligned with wealth. I am abundant now." Say it with strength until your body believes it.
- Meditation: Sit with your ticket or with empty hands. Visualize beams of light filling you, connecting you to universal abundance. See the wealth flowing into your life without struggle.

Reframing "Losing" as Alignment Training

Not every draw will deliver you millions, but every ticket can deliver alignment. If you call it a loss, you pull your energy into regret, remorse, and lack. But if you call it an investment in your alignment, you stay connected.

Think of it this way:

- You did not lose—you strengthened your vibration.
- You did not waste—you practiced commanding wealth.
- You did not fail—you built spiritual stamina.

Every time you reframe, you stay high in frequency. Excitement grows instead of shrinking. That excitement is the magnet that draws the jackpot closer.

So say: "I never lose. I only align closer to my win."

Daily Lotto Affirmations

1. I am already holding the winning ticket in my spirit.
2. I see my millions, and I welcome them now.
3. I am aligned with Mega Millions, Powerball, and every jackpot.
4. My ticket is stamped with divine favor.
5. Abundance flows into my life with ease and certainty.
6. I win every time I play because I am always aligned.
7. My millions are here, and I receive them joyfully.

Game-Winning Affirmations

1. Victory is my nature—I win in every arena.
2. Every game bends to my favor because I am aligned.
3. I attract winning outcomes in all I do.
4. Triumph is my frequency; success is my reality.
5. I play with joy, and joy multiplies my blessings.
6. Winning is my normal, my constant, my flow.
7. I am a champion in mind, spirit, and life.

Declaration of Alignment

"I visualize my win, I breathe into my win, I meditate on my win, I declare my win. I do not lose—I align. Every ticket brings me closer, every draw strengthens my certainty. I am the jackpot winner in energy, in vision, and in truth. I am always connected, always aligned, always abundant."

The Alignment Treatment (Ritual)
Before You Play

Step 1 — Prepare Your Space

- Sit somewhere quiet, free from distractions.
- Hold your ticket, or if you don't yet have one, hold your empty hands as if the ticket is already there.
- Place your feet flat on the ground, grounding yourself in stability.

Step 2 — Breathwork of Abundance

- Inhale deeply for 7 counts, saying silently: "I receive abundance."
- Hold your breath for 4 counts, saying: "I seal abundance."
- Exhale slowly for 8 counts, saying: "I release lack."
- Repeat 3 times until your body feels calm and charged with energy.

Step 3 — Visualization

- Close your eyes and see yourself holding the winning ticket.
- Imagine the numbers shining with golden light.
- Picture yourself smiling, celebrating, giving thanks, and feeling secure.
- See what you'll do next: hugging your loved ones, calling your lawyer, or depositing your check.

Step 4 — Declarations

Speak these out loud, with certainty:

- "I am the jackpot winner."
- "I have the winning ticket."
- "I am aligned with wealth, and wealth is aligned with me."

Step 5 — Reframe Any "Loss"

Before you even play, set your mindset:

- "No matter the outcome, I never lose—I align."
- "Every ticket is an investment in my vibration."
- "Each play brings me closer to the jackpot already mine."

Step 6 — Closing Gratitude

- Place your hand on your heart.
- Whisper: "Thank you for my millions. Thank you for my abundance. Thank you for my certainty."
- Smile, because gratitude is the proof of already having.

This treatment (ritual) keeps the energy high, removes desperation, and makes playing a sacred act of alignment.

TO DO LIST

DATE: ____________________ DUE DATE ____________________

TO DO

- [ ] ____________________
- [ ] ____________________
- [ ] ____________________
- [ ] ____________________
- [ ] ____________________
- [ ] ____________________
- [ ] ____________________
- [ ] ____________________
- [ ] ____________________
- [ ] ____________________
- [ ] ____________________
- [ ] ____________________
- [ ] ____________________
- [ ] ____________________
- [ ] ____________________
- [ ] ____________________
- [ ] ____________________
- [ ] ____________________
- [ ] ____________________
- [ ] ____________________
- [ ] ____________________
- [ ] ____________________
- [ ] ____________________
- [ ] ____________________
- [ ] ____________________
- [ ] ____________________

PRIORITIES

- [ ] ____________________
- [ ] ____________________
- [ ] ____________________
- [ ] ____________________
- [ ] ____________________
- [ ] ____________________
- [ ] ____________________

NOTES

REMINDER

Notes

Chapter 3 – Preparing for the Win (The Winner's List)

Chapter 3 — Preparing for the Win (The Winner's List)

Why Preparation Matters

Most people think, "When I win, then I'll figure it out." That is the biggest trap. The truth is, when millions suddenly land in your lap, you will be overwhelmed—your emotions will be racing, everyone around you will change, and opportunists will appear overnight. If you wait until that moment to start planning, you'll be scrambling, and scrambling is how people lose money, relationships, and peace.

Preparation is protection. Just like you keep an emergency bag ready for fire or disaster, you need a Wealth Emergency Bag—a list of steps, names, and strategies already written down. That way, when the numbers align in your favor, you won't panic. You'll already know: "Here's who I call. Here's where I go. Here's how I secure my win."

Start Now, Not Later

You don't need to be a millionaire to start preparing like one. Some steps cost nothing but time, research, and wisdom.

For example:

- You can start researching lawyers in your state now and keep their business cards.

- You can research banks, FDIC limits, and options for accounts.
- You can write down your goals for where you would live, who you would support, and how you would grow your wealth.
- You can begin the process of opening a trust, even if it doesn't yet hold millions.
- You can make a list of people you trust—and just as importantly, those you don't.

Preparation is not about investing (spending) money you don't have. It's about mapping out the steps so you don't waste time when the door opens.

Chapter 3 — Preparing for the Win (The Winner's List)

The Winner's List — Expanded

1. Legal & Financial Protection
   - Hire a lottery lawyer (specialized in anonymity and protection).
   - Hire a tax strategist (to reduce tax burdens legally).
   - Decide how to receive winnings: lump sum vs. annuity.
   - Consider offshore accounts or international diversification for added protection.
   - Draft confidentiality agreements for staff, family, or anyone who may know of your winnings.

2. Living & Lifestyle
   - Decide your primary residence (city, country, coast, or abroad).
   - Purchase a safe property with security systems.
   - Acquire a second/vacation home for rest and retreat.
   - Build or rent a private office/studio for creative or business pursuits.
   - Consider personal protection (security detail, if needed).

3. Health & Wellbeing
   - Full medical check-up after receiving wealth.
   - Long-term therapy or coaching to process sudden life changes.
   - Upgrade mental health care (stress management, meditation training).
   - Explore longevity practices (herbalists, advanced medicine, holistic treatments).

4. Family & Legacy
- Create inheritance plans that prevent disputes.
- Fund scholarships or grants in your family's name.
- Support elderly relatives with housing, healthcare, or caretakers.
- Record family history (document elders' wisdom, preserve culture).
- Consider adoption, fostering, or mentoring programs if aligned.

5. Contribution & Expansion
- Start or invest in sustainable businesses (farms, schools, wellness centers).
- Launch a foundation for causes that matter to you.
- Support arts, culture, and spirituality (museums, temples, retreats).
- Create generational wealth structures (trusts, LLCs, land ownership).

6. Personal Development & Education (often missed!)
- Go back to school for fun or passion projects.
- Take courses in financial literacy, real estate, entrepreneurship.
- Travel to learn languages, cultures, and wisdom traditions.
- Hire mentors and coaches to expand your vision.

7. Privacy & Safety (the most forgotten piece)
- Change phone numbers, emails, and strengthen digital security.

- Keep your name off public records (use trusts/LLCs).
- Limit who knows about your winnings—protect from opportunists.
- Relocate quietly if needed to ensure safety and peace.

By adding personal growth, safety/privacy, and long-term expansion, the Winner's List becomes a complete blueprint for transforming sudden wealth into lifelong abundance and peace.

The Winner's List (example)

Think of this as your private notebook, your step-by-step manual for the day you wake up and see your numbers called. Your list may include:

1. Legal & Financial Protection
    - List of 2–3 trusted lawyers in your state who specialize in wealth, estates, and lottery law.
    - A shortlist of accountants and tax strategists.
    - Bank research: which banks to use, and how much FDIC covers.
    - Note: lump sum vs. annuity payout—know the difference before you win.
    - Draft ideas for trusts, LLCs, or estate planning.

2. Living & Lifestyle
    - Where you'd like to live if you moved: city, countryside, gated community, or abroad.
    - A list of neighborhoods you feel safe in.
    - Notes on upgrading wardrobe, car, or security when the time is right.
    - Assistants or staff you might want (house manager, personal assistant, chef, etc.).

3. Health & Wellbeing
    - A health upgrade list: dentist, dermatologist, nutritionist, therapist, fitness coach.
    - Holistic options: acupuncturist, meditation teacher, energy healer.
    - A personal vision of how you want to feel and look after wealth flows in.

4. Family & Legacy

- Who you want to support (parents, siblings, children, nieces, nephews).
- Education plans (scholarships, tuition, or training for family).
- How you'll honor ancestors (land, memorials, libations).
- Family inheritance structure: who gets what and how.

5. Contribution & Expansion

- Causes and charities that matter most to you.
- Business ideas you'd invest in or create.
- Community projects you'd like to support.
- Cultural or spiritual projects to leave as legacy.

6. Privacy & Safety

- Change of phone numbers, emails, and digital security plans.
- How to protect your name in public (trusts, LLCs).
- Who you would tell—and who you would not.
- Notes on personal safety: relocation, bodyguards, or anonymity if necessary.

Revisit and Upgrade Your List

This is not a one-time exercise. Life changes, laws change, people change. Just as you upgrade your wardrobe or your phone, you must upgrade your Winner's List. Review it every few months. Add new names, remove untrustworthy people, refine your vision. The more you refine, the stronger your alignment.

Affirmations for Preparation

1. I am always prepared for wealth to find me.
2. My list is ready, my mind is ready, my spirit is ready.
3. I am ten steps ahead of those who would try to use me.
4. Preparation is my protection, and it multiplies my blessings.
5. I am wise enough to plan, and powerful enough to receive.

Declaration of Readiness

"I will not wait until millions are in my hands to become wise. I prepare now. I plan now. I secure my future now. My Winner's List is my emergency bag, my guide, and my shield. When the day comes, I will not panic. I will act with clarity, confidence, and power. I am already prepared, and that is why I am already a winner."

The whole point here is crystal clear: don't wait until the blessing comes—live prepared.

Chapter 3 — Preparing for the Win (The Winner's List)

Sample Winner's List (Example)

Here's what a filled-in Winner's List might look like for someone preparing today.

1. Legal & Financial Protection
    - Lottery lawyer: Attorney Jean Woule (business card on file).
    - Accountant/Tax strategist: Marie Dieugrand CPA.
    - Bank choice: Janah Bank Private Client account + Credit Union backup.
    - Estate plan: Start trust next year with $5,000.

2. Living & Lifestyle
    - Dream area: Gated community in Atlanta suburbs.
    - Car upgrade: Tesla Model X.
    - Wardrobe: Hire a personal stylist for a new look.

3. Health & Wellbeing
    - Dentist: Dr. Carter (already have contact).
    - Dermatologist: Dr. Shah (consult scheduled next month).
    - Fitness: Yoga twice a week + walking group.

4. Family & Legacy
    - Parents: Buy them a house.
    - Niece & nephew: Create education trust funds.
    - Ancestors: Build memorial garden on family land.

5. Contribution & Expansion

- Business: Open wellness retreat center.
- Charity: Donate $50k annually to orphanage.
- Legacy: Scholarship fund in grandmother's name.

6. Privacy & Safety

- Change phone number & emails.
- LLC ownership for house purchase.
- Only tell immediate family.

Journal Prompts: Build Your Own Winner's List

- Who are the first three people I would call if I won? Should they be on my "safe" list or not?
- What debts or obligations do I need to clear before stepping into new wealth?
- Where would I live if safety and money were no issue?
- What doctors, healers, or coaches would I invest in to upgrade my health?
- Which charities, causes, or organizations would I support?
- Who in my family deserves long-term support, and how can I structure it so it lasts?
- How can I protect my privacy and safety from opportunists?

Mini Treatment (Ritual): Writing Your Winner's List

1. Sit with a notebook dedicated only to your Winner's List.
2. Light a candle (or sit in natural light) and say: "I am preparing for my wealth with wisdom."
3. Write each category clearly (Legal, Lifestyle, Health, Family, Contribution, Safety).
4. Fill in names, places, or ideas you already know. Leave space for updates.
5. After writing, place your hand over the notebook and declare:
6. "This list is my guide, my emergency bag, and my protection. I am prepared, I am wise, I am ready."
7. Revisit your list every few months and refine it.

TO DO LIST

DATE: ____________ DUE DATE ____________

TO DO

- [ ] ____
- [ ] ____
- [ ] ____
- [ ] ____
- [ ] ____
- [ ] ____
- [ ] ____
- [ ] ____
- [ ] ____
- [ ] ____
- [ ] ____
- [ ] ____
- [ ] ____
- [ ] ____
- [ ] ____
- [ ] ____
- [ ] ____
- [ ] ____
- [ ] ____
- [ ] ____
- [ ] ____
- [ ] ____
- [ ] ____
- [ ] ____
- [ ] ____
- [ ] ____

PRIORITIES

- [ ] ____
- [ ] ____
- [ ] ____
- [ ] ____
- [ ] ____
- [ ] ____
- [ ] ____

NOTES

REMINDER

Notes

Chapter 4 – The First 72 Hours After Winning

Chapter 4 — The First 72 Hours After Winning

The Shock and the Stillness

When you first see those winning numbers match your ticket, your body may tremble, your heart may race, and your mind may spin. You may feel like screaming, crying, or calling everyone you know. But the truth is—your first act is not to shout. Your first act is to breathe.

Wealth changes everything. In those first hours, you must anchor yourself before anyone else anchors you.

Step 1 — Stay Quiet, Breathe, Center Yourself

- Do not announce it publicly.
- Do not rush to social media.
- Do not call ten friends or family members.

Instead, breathe. Sit quietly. Allow yourself to absorb the truth. The calmer you are in those first hours, the more power you hold moving forward.

Step 2 — Secure the Ticket

- Sign the back of your ticket immediately (legally, it protects ownership).
- Place it in a waterproof, fireproof safe or safety deposit box.
- Take photos and copies for your private records, but keep them hidden.

Remember: the ticket is not paper—it is a key to your new life. Treat it as sacred.

Step 3 — Spiritual Grounding (Optional but Powerful)

If you are a spiritual person, the first hours should include grounding practices:

- Say a prayer of gratitude.
- Pour libations to ancestors who walked before you.
- Meditate or journal your thanks.
- Light a candle and declare:

"I receive this blessing with wisdom and protection."

Gratitude anchors wealth. It keeps your heart aligned with purpose, not ego.

Step 4 — Decide Who You Can Truly Trust

This is not the time to test people's loyalty. You must already have your Winner's List (from Chapter 3) prepared. Decide from that list:

- Who you can safely tell.
- Who must never know.
- Who is part of your immediate circle of protection.

Even well-meaning family can betray you out of greed, jealousy, or pressure. Protect yourself first.

Step 5 — Safety First in Celebration

Many winners make the mistake of celebrating recklessly: going to bars, partying with strangers, or indulging in drugs. These choices make you visible, vulnerable, and unsafe.

- If you celebrate, do it quietly, privately, and safely.
- Surround yourself with only the most trusted people.
- Avoid large crowds and unnecessary attention.

Remember: the minute you become a winner, you also become a target. Protect your life before you protect your money.

Step 6 — Learn From Sad Stories

There are countless tragic stories of lottery winners who:

- Were betrayed by spouses.
- Were set up by friends.
- Were robbed or harmed by strangers.
- Lost everything to bad investments.

These are not meant to scare you—they are meant to prepare you. Study their mistakes so you do not repeat them. Be humble, be alert, be wise.

Affirmations for the First 72 Hours

1. I breathe, I center, I stay calm in my power.
2. My ticket is safe, my spirit is safe, my wealth is safe.
3. I choose gratitude before I choose action.
4. I celebrate with wisdom, not recklessness.
5. I am protected, guided, and favored in my next steps.
6. I move in silence and strength.
7. My first 72 hours create a lifetime of stability.

Declaration of Calm Victory

"I do not rush. I do not panic. I do not expose myself. I breathe. I ground. I give thanks. I move wisely. My ticket is safe, my soul is safe, my destiny is safe. I am a winner not just because I hold the numbers, but because I hold wisdom. My first steps are calm, powerful, and protected. Nothing and no one can shake me."

It gives both the sacred grounding and the protective warnings so you know what to do immediately after winning.

Too often, winners rush to give, to prove, to please, forgetting that their first responsibility is to themselves. Safety, grounding, and self-celebration come before sharing with anyone else. This "Sacred Vow of Self-Priority" can be spoken daily in those first 72 hours, and even beyond.

The Sacred Vow of Self-Priority

"I vow to put myself first.
I vow to protect my safety above all.
I vow to celebrate with myself before
I share with anyone else.
I vow to move in wisdom, not guilt.
I vow to be unapologetic about my security,
my peace, and my well-being.
I vow to honor this blessing by honoring myself first.
Because if I am not safe,
no one connected to me will be safe.
I am the vessel, and I must guard the vessel.
This vow is my shield, my reminder, and my truth:
I come first, and through my safety, everything else flows."

This is to give you a mantra of protection and self-anchoring. It reprograms you away from guilt or the urge to rush and give to others before securing themselves.

7 Mantras of Protection & Self-Priority

1. "My safety comes first, and I owe no one an apology for protecting myself."
2. "I cannot pour into others before I fill my own cup."
3. "I celebrate with myself first, for I am the vessel of this blessing."
4. "Guilt has no place in my abundance; I move only with wisdom and peace."
5. "I am not obligated to anyone's demands—I choose how and when I give."
6. "My wealth is sacred, and I protect it by protecting myself."
7. "By honoring myself first, I ensure that my blessings flow safely to others."

These mantras anchor you in self-preservation, guilt-free abundance, and unapologetic protection.

TO DO LIST

DATE: ____________ DUE DATE ____________

TO DO

- ☐ ____________
- ☐ ____________
- ☐ ____________
- ☐ ____________
- ☐ ____________
- ☐ ____________
- ☐ ____________
- ☐ ____________
- ☐ ____________
- ☐ ____________
- ☐ ____________
- ☐ ____________
- ☐ ____________
- ☐ ____________
- ☐ ____________
- ☐ ____________
- ☐ ____________
- ☐ ____________
- ☐ ____________
- ☐ ____________
- ☐ ____________
- ☐ ____________
- ☐ ____________
- ☐ ____________
- ☐ ____________
- ☐ ____________

PRIORITIES

- ☐ ____________
- ☐ ____________
- ☐ ____________
- ☐ ____________
- ☐ ____________
- ☐ ____________
- ☐ ____________

NOTES

REMINDER

Notes

Chapter 5 – Maintaining Wealth, Not Returning to Poverty

Chapter 5 is where we shift from the immediate response of winning into the long-term consciousness of sustaining wealth. It's not just about keeping money, but about training the mind and spirit to never return to poverty. So stay focused on that goal. Always remember that you're able, and you can do this.

Chapter 5 — Maintaining Wealth, Not Returning to Poverty

The Millionaire Mindset vs. the Poverty Mindset

Money alone does not change you—it amplifies who you already are. That's why some winners go broke within years, while others multiply their blessings. The difference is mindset.

- Poverty mindset fears money will run out. It spends recklessly, gives without boundaries, or hoards out of fear. Poverty mindset thinks short-term: "What can I buy now?"
- Millionaire mindset knows money flows and multiplies. It plans, invests, and protects. It sets boundaries around giving, so generosity is sustainable. Millionaire mindset thinks long-term: "How can I make this last for generations?"

If you do not shift into millionaire thinking, you will eventually sink back into the same patterns that kept you limited before.

Master Manifestor Language: From "I Need" to "I Have"

Language is power. Every word you speak is a command to your subconscious and to the universe.

- "I need" vibrates with lack. It says you are empty and desperate.
- "I want" vibrates with longing. It says you are reaching but not yet receiving.
- "I am" vibrates with identity. It says you are already the thing you seek.
- "I have" vibrates with possession. It says the blessing is already in your hands.

To maintain wealth, you must speak as if it is permanent:

- Not "I hope this lasts," but "I have lasting wealth."
- Not "I don't want to lose it," but "I have wisdom to grow it."
- Not "I'm afraid of going broke," but "I have security, expansion, and overflow."

Winners keep winning because they speak like masters.

How to Invest and Grow Wealth

Money that sits will eventually shrink. Inflation, taxes, and poor planning eat it away. To maintain wealth, you must make your money work harder than you do.

- Invest in property: Land, real estate, and housing are long-term security.
- Invest in businesses: Choose industries you understand, or hire experts.
- Invest in markets: Stocks, bonds, or funds—but only with guidance from trustworthy advisors.
- Invest in self: Courses, mentors, spiritual growth, therapy—wealth in the mind keeps wealth in the bank.

Growth comes when you see money as a tool, not a trophy.

Schools, Businesses, Spiritual Investments

Wealth is not only for you—it is also for the world around you. A true millionaire mindset asks: "What will I build that outlives me?"

- Schools: Fund education programs, scholarships, or community learning centers.
- Businesses: Create jobs and opportunities that uplift others.
- Spiritual investments: Support temples, cultural centers, or healing spaces that nourish generations.
- Legacy projects: Write books, record wisdom, build foundations that carry your name with honor.
- These investments feed not only your pockets but your soul.

How to Live Richly and Responsibly

Wealth does not mean recklessness—it means richness in every sense.

- Live richly by upgrading your health, environment, and daily joy.
- Live responsibly by protecting your money, your peace, and your privacy.
- Give with wisdom: don't let guilt force you into bankruptcy.
- Maintain balance: enjoy luxury but never abandon discipline.

The true goal is not just to win once—it is to never return to where you started.

Affirmations for Sustained Wealth

1. I have lasting wealth that multiplies daily.
2. I live with wisdom, discipline, and joy.
3. My money grows because I grow in mindset.
4. I am trusted with wealth, and I use it with clarity.
5. I am not afraid of loss; I am aligned with increase.
6. I have investments that expand my legacy.
7. I live richly, responsibly, and abundantly.

Declaration of Permanent Abundance

"I will never return to poverty, lack, or desperation. I shift from wanting to having, from fearing to securing, from short-term thrills to long-term wealth. My money multiplies because I multiply in wisdom. My wealth is permanent, my abundance is infinite, my legacy is secured. I live richly, I live responsibly, and I live forever abundant."

Mistakes That Drain Wealth

Many lottery winners and sudden millionaires lose everything within years because they were unprepared. Awareness of these traps will protect you from repeating their mistakes.

1. Overspending (overinvesting) on Luxury (remember spending is an invesment so everytime you must invest wisely).

- Buying too many cars, houses, or clothes too quickly.
- Remember: wealth is not about how much you spend, but how much you sustain.

2. Giving Without Boundaries

- Handing out money to friends, family, or strangers out of guilt.
- True generosity is structured, not impulsive. Give with wisdom, not emotion.

3. Poor Investments

- Jumping into businesses you don't understand.
- Trusting get-rich-quick schemes or shady "advisors."
- Always research, verify, and move with caution.

4. Ignoring Taxes

- Forgetting that taxes can take nearly half your winnings.
- Without a tax strategist, you risk penalties or losing millions.

5. No Privacy or Protection

- Announcing your win publicly.
- Living too loudly or without security.
- Wealth attracts attention—both good and bad.

6. Not Upgrading the Mindset

- Keeping old habits of lack, fear, or recklessness.
- If your mind does not change, your wealth cannot last.

Protective Mantra

"I am disciplined. I am wise. I protect my money from waste, greed, and foolishness. My wealth multiplies because I move with clarity, caution, and vision."

This chapter (5) isn't only about money management, it's about sustaining wealth through personal growth and support systems. If we leave it out, you, or other readers, might think wealth is just numbers and investments, when in reality it's also emotional stability, spiritual grounding, and social refinement. Lastly, Chapter 5 is also holistic and strong: mindset, money, mistakes to avoid, and mentors to trust.

Spiritual, Personal, and Social Guidance

Wealth is not just financial—it is emotional, spiritual, and social. To maintain wealth, you must also maintain yourself. Sudden money can bring stress, isolation, or pressure you've never experienced before. That's why having trusted guides in place is essential.

Spiritual Leader or Counselor:

- Someone who can keep you grounded in gratitude, prayer, or meditation. Money magnifies your life, but spirit keeps it steady. Start building relationships now with leaders you respect, so when you win, you already know who you can lean on.

Personal Coach or Therapist:

- A coach can guide your mindset, keep you focused, and help you navigate the emotional highs and lows of sudden wealth. A therapist can help process family dynamics, betrayal, or stress that often follows winning.

Etiquette and Social Coaching:

- Wealth changes your circles. You may be invited to spaces where etiquette, refinement, and presentation matter. An etiquette coach can help you move with confidence and grace, so you are never intimidated or out of place.

Don’t wait until after you win to seek guidance. Begin now—test the waters, build connections, and learn who you can trust. Wealth without wisdom is a curse, but wealth with guidance becomes a blessing that lasts generations.

Chapter 5 is so powerful, let's review it again (because practice will make you better).

Chapter 5 — Maintaining Wealth, Not Returning to Poverty

The Millionaire Mindset vs. the Poverty Mindset

Winning millions does not guarantee keeping millions. Money is a mirror—it only reflects who you are. That is why some winners multiply their blessings while others lose everything within years.

The difference is mindset.

- Poverty mindset fears money will run out. It spends recklessly, gives without boundaries, or hoards in panic. It focuses on the short-term: "What can I buy today?"
- Millionaire mindset knows money is a tool that multiplies when guided with wisdom. It protects, invests, and plans. It gives with intention, not guilt. It focuses on the long-term: "How can I build wealth that lasts generations?"

If your mind does not shift, your money cannot stay.

Master Manifestor Language:
From "I Need" to "I Have"
Your words are spiritual contracts. Every sentence you speak programs your subconscious and sends instructions into the universe.

- "I need" is a vibration of lack—it keeps you in survival.
- "I want" is a vibration of longing—it keeps you reaching but never receiving.
- "I am" is a vibration of identity—it claims power in the present.
- "I have" is a vibration of possession—it anchors wealth as permanent.

To maintain your abundance, you must shift into the language of already having: Not "I hope this lasts," but "I have lasting wealth."

- Not "I don't want to go broke," but "I have stability and overflow."
- Not "I'm afraid to lose it," but "I have wisdom that grows wealth daily."

How to Invest and Grow Wealth

Money that sits shrinks. Inflation, taxes, and poor choices will eat it away. True abundance grows because it is put to work.

- Property: Land, real estate, and housing are foundations of security.
- Businesses: Invest in industries you understand or with trusted advisors.
- Markets: Stocks, bonds, or funds—but never without guidance.

- Self-Investment: Courses, mentors, spiritual growth, therapy, and education—because your wealth can only expand as far as your mind.

Wealth is not a trophy; it is a tool.

Schools, Businesses, Spiritual Investments

Lasting wealth builds legacy. Ask yourself:
What will I create that will live after me?

- Schools: Fund education, scholarships, or mentorship programs.
- Businesses: Create jobs and opportunities that uplift others.
- Spiritual Investments: Build healing centers, cultural spaces, or retreats that restore souls.
- Legacy Projects: Write books, record your wisdom, plant seeds that bear fruit for generations.

Wealth is richest when it outlives you.

Spiritual, Personal, and Social Guidance

Wealth is not only financial—it is emotional, spiritual, and social. Sudden money can bring stress, isolation, and pressures you never imagined. That is why you must prepare support systems now.

- Spiritual Leader or Counselor: Someone who keeps you grounded in gratitude, prayer, or meditation. Start developing trust now, so when the money comes, you already know who holds you steady.
- Personal Coach or Therapist: To help navigate new emotions, relationships, and choices. Wealth without emotional maturity can be dangerous.
- Etiquette and Social Coaching: New circles may require new confidence. Learning refined skills ensures you walk in any room with ease and authority.

Do not wait until the millions arrive—begin building these connections today.

Mistakes That Drain Wealth

Learn from those who lost it all. Their mistakes are warnings, not destiny.

1. Overspending on Luxury: Buying cars, homes, and clothes without planning.
2. Giving Without Boundaries: Handing out money recklessly to family or friends out of guilt.
3. Poor Investments: Rushing into businesses or trusting shady "advisors."
4. Ignoring Taxes: Forgetting that taxes can take nearly half your winnings.
5. No Privacy or Protection: Living loudly, exposing your win, or neglecting safety.
6. Not Upgrading the Mindset: Clinging to old habits of fear or lack.

How to Live Richly and Responsibly

To live richly is to embrace joy, health, beauty, and peace. To live responsibly is to guard your abundance with wisdom.

- Upgrade your environment, health, and self-care.
- Enjoy luxury without abandoning discipline.
- Give generously but within safe boundaries.
- Protect your peace by living intentionally and privately.

The true goal is not just to win once—but to never return to where you were.

Affirmations for Sustained Wealth

1. I have wealth that multiplies with wisdom.
2. I live richly, responsibly, and securely.
3. My money works for me and grows daily.
4. I am trusted with abundance and use it wisely.
5. I am safe, disciplined, and favored in wealth.
6. I have investments that expand my legacy.
7. My abundance is permanent and generational.

Declaration of Permanent Abundance

"I will never return to poverty, lack, or desperation. I shift from wanting to having, from fearing to securing, from short-term thrills to long-term legacy. My money multiplies because I multiply in wisdom. My wealth is permanent, my abundance is infinite, my legacy is secured. I live richly, responsibly, and forever abundant."

TO DO LIST

DATE: ____________ DUE DATE ____________

TO DO

- [ ]
- [ ]
- [ ]
- [ ]
- [ ]
- [ ]
- [ ]
- [ ]
- [ ]
- [ ]
- [ ]
- [ ]
- [ ]
- [ ]
- [ ]
- [ ]
- [ ]
- [ ]
- [ ]
- [ ]
- [ ]
- [ ]
- [ ]
- [ ]
- [ ]
- [ ]

PRIORITIES

- [ ]
- [ ]
- [ ]
- [ ]
- [ ]
- [ ]
- [ ]

NOTES

REMINDER

Notes

Chapter 6 – Affirmations for Winners Only

— Chapter 6 is there we gather the pure power words that seal everything from the earlier chapters. This is the treasure chest of affirmations and declarations where you can come back to every day. So be sure to use that to your advantage.

Chapter 6 — Affirmations for Winners Only

Affirmations are the language of certainty. They are not wishes, they are commands. When spoken with conviction, they reprogram the subconscious, align the spirit, and magnetize reality. Speak these words daily. Speak them before you play, after you win, and even when you are simply living.

Lotto Affirmations (I Already Have the Millions)

1. I already have the winning ticket in my hands.
2. I have the Mega Millions, I have the Powerball, I have the jackpot.
3. I am the chosen winner, and my millions are secure.
4. The numbers align perfectly with my destiny.
5. My wealth is guaranteed, and I walk in it now.
6. I do not wait—I already have it.
7. My millions are here, sealed and delivered.

Jackpot Declarations

1. "I am crowned the jackpot winner—wealth bows before me."
2. "My numbers shine with golden light; fortune aligns with my spirit."
3. "I declare that abundance flows into my life in unstoppable streams."
4. "I am the vessel chosen for this overflow, and I handle it with wisdom."
5. "Every draw, every game, every chance bends toward my victory."
6. "The jackpot is mine by divine right, by universal law, and by certainty."
7. "I celebrate now because the win is already done."

Abundance Affirmations for Everyday Wealth

- I have more than enough for every need and every dream.
- Money flows to me in endless streams of blessing.
- I attract wealth from all directions, seen and unseen.
- Opportunities, investments, and favor multiply daily in my life.
- I am aligned with prosperity in business, career, and creativity.
- My bank accounts overflow with stability and growth.
- Abundance is my normal, my constant, my way of life.

Health, Love, and Legacy Affirmations

Money supports, but it does not replace the things that make life whole. Wealth must strengthen your health, your love, and your legacy.

Health Affirmations

1. I have radiant health, and I invest in my body with care.
2. My wealth supports my healing, fitness, and longevity.
3. I have vitality, strength, and peace in my body daily.

Love Affirmations

1. I am surrounded by love that cannot be bought or broken.
2. I attract relationships that honor my soul, not just my money.
3. I have loyalty, trust, and joy in love.

Legacy Affirmations

1. I have a legacy that blesses generations after me.
2. My wealth builds schools, businesses, and sacred spaces.
3. I have wisdom that multiplies wealth beyond money —I pass down truth, courage, and power.

Closing Declaration of a True Winner

"I am the jackpot winner, the wealth holder, the abundance carrier. I already have the millions, I already have the blessings, I already have the overflow. My wealth is permanent, my health is radiant, my love is sacred, and my legacy is eternal. I do not chase;

I claim. I do not beg; I have. I am aligned, I am favored, I am rich—in spirit, in money, in love, and in destiny. So it is, and so it must be."

We want you to know that, with this chapter, you now hold a book of power words they can use as a daily shield and magnet.

A "Winner's Vow" — is something sacred, strong, and unforgettable. This will serve as a personal covenant for you where you can repeat daily to seal your identity as winners in every sense, not just financially.

We fortify this Chapter (6) so it becomes the ultimate powerhouse for every winner, especially winners like you.

1. An Incantation for Winners (long, rhythmic, spell-like).
2. 7 Mantras for Winners (short, punchy, repeatable anytime).
3. The Winner's Vow (sacred, sealing covenant).

The Winner's Incantation

Speak this slowly, with rhythm and breath, like you're commanding the universe:

"I am the chosen.
I am the crowned.
I am the jackpot walking,
the abundance living, the legacy breathing.
Numbers bend to me, wealth bows to me,
overflow runs toward me.
I am not waiting—I have it.
I am not hoping—I hold it.
I am not begging—I command it.
Every dollar, every blessing,
every door opens for me.
I am the master of wealth,
the guardian of abundance,
the vessel of legacy.

So it is, so it must be, so it already is."

7 Mantras for Winners

1. I already have it.
2. Wealth is my natural state.
3. I am chosen to win.
4. Money obeys my energy.
5. I celebrate my abundance daily.
6. My legacy is secured.
7. I remain a winner forever.

The Winner's Vow

"I vow to think, speak, and act as a winner in all things.
I vow to honor my wealth, my health,
my love, and my legacy.

I vow to live in the language of I am and I have,
never in lack, fear, or desperation.

I vow to protect my abundance with
wisdom, discipline, and clarity.

I vow to rise above guilt, manipulation, and distraction.
I vow to use my winnings to secure myself,
bless my loved ones, and uplift my world.

I vow to never shrink, never beg, never doubt
—I am a winner, and I remain a winner.

This vow is sacred, sealed, and unbreakable.

I am the jackpot.
I am the blessing.
I am the abundance.

So it is, and so it will forever be."

The Winner's Vow (repeat in case one does not read in script)

"I vow to think, speak,
and act as a winner in all things.
I vow to honor my wealth, my health,
my love, and my legacy.
I vow to live in the language of
I am and I have, never in lack,
fear, or desperation.
I vow to protect my abundance
with wisdom, discipline, and clarity.

I vow to rise above guilt,
manipulation, and distraction.
I vow to use my winnings
to secure myself, bless my loved ones,
and uplift my world.

I vow to never shrink,
never beg, never doubt—I am a winner,
and I remain a winner.

This vow is sacred, sealed,
and unbreakable.

I am the jackpot.
I am the blessing.
I am the abundance.

So it is, and so it will forever be."

With these three closing pieces, Chapter 6 is certainly a fortress of words made just for this moment—affirmations, declarations, an incantation, mantras, and the vow. So be sure to use them wisely. Just take it one day at a time, no rush.

Let's reaffirm again on the next page, this is a (continuous) powerhouse.

Chapter 6 — Triple Lock of Power
(let's review & repeat again)

A) Winner Affirmations (repeat daily)

1. I already have the winning ticket.
2. I have the Mega Millions. I have the Powerball.
3. I am chosen to win; my millions are secured.
4. Money obeys my energy and multiplies for me.
5. I have permanent, generational wealth.
6. I am safe, guided, and wise with abundance.
7. My investments grow while I sleep.
8. I celebrate quietly, protect fiercely, give wisely.
9. I have radiant health, sacred love, and lasting peace.
10. My legacy blesses those after me.
11. I am the jackpot walking—overflow follows me.
12. So it is, because I have it now.

B) Closing Declaration

"I am the jackpot winner, the wealth holder,
the abundance carrier.
I already have the millions, the favor, the overflow.
My wealth is permanent, my health is radiant,
my love is sacred, and my legacy is eternal.
I do not chase; I claim. I do not beg; I have.
I live aligned, protected, disciplined, and joyful.
So it is, and so it must be."

C) The Winner's Vow (for winners only) (Keep reviewing, repeating this until it sinks into your subconscious mind)

"I vow to think, speak, and
act as a winner in all things.
I vow to honor my wealth,
my health, my love, and my legacy.
I vow to live in the language of
I am and I have,
never in lack, fear, or desperation.
I vow to protect my abundance
with wisdom, discipline, and clarity.
I vow to rise above guilt, manipulation,
and distraction.
I vow to use my winnings to secure myself,
bless my loved ones, and uplift my world.
I vow to never shrink,
never beg, never doubt
—I am a winner, and
I remain a winner.
This vow is sacred, sealed,
and unbreakable.
I am the jackpot.
I am the blessing.
I am the abundance.
So it is, and so it will forever be."

Bonus: Incantation & 7 Mantras

Winner's Incantation (Repeat)

"I am the chosen.
I am the crowned.
I am the jackpot walking,
the abundance living,
the legacy breathing.
Numbers bend to me,
wealth bows to me,
overflow runs toward me.
I am not waiting—I have it.
I am not hoping—I hold it.
I am not begging—I command it.
Every dollar, every blessing,
every door opens for me.
I am the master of wealth,
the guardian of abundance,
the vessel of legacy.
So it is, so it must be, so it already is."

7 Mantras for Winners

1. I already have it.
2. Wealth is my natural state.
3. I am chosen to win.
4. Money obeys my energy.
5. I celebrate my abundance daily.
6. My legacy is secured.
7. I remain a winner forever.

TO DO LIST

DATE: ____________ DUE DATE ____________

TO DO

- ☐ ____________
- ☐ ____________
- ☐ ____________
- ☐ ____________
- ☐ ____________
- ☐ ____________
- ☐ ____________
- ☐ ____________
- ☐ ____________
- ☐ ____________
- ☐ ____________
- ☐ ____________
- ☐ ____________
- ☐ ____________
- ☐ ____________
- ☐ ____________
- ☐ ____________
- ☐ ____________
- ☐ ____________
- ☐ ____________
- ☐ ____________
- ☐ ____________
- ☐ ____________
- ☐ ____________
- ☐ ____________
- ☐ ____________

PRIORITIES

- ☐ ____________
- ☐ ____________
- ☐ ____________
- ☐ ____________
- ☐ ____________
- ☐ ____________
- ☐ ____________

NOTES

REMINDER

Notes

TO DO LIST

DATE: ____________________ DUE DATE ____________________

TO DO

☐ ____________________
☐ ____________________
☐ ____________________
☐ ____________________
☐ ____________________
☐ ____________________
☐ ____________________
☐ ____________________
☐ ____________________
☐ ____________________
☐ ____________________
☐ ____________________
☐ ____________________
☐ ____________________
☐ ____________________
☐ ____________________
☐ ____________________
☐ ____________________
☐ ____________________
☐ ____________________
☐ ____________________
☐ ____________________
☐ ____________________
☐ ____________________
☐ ____________________
☐ ____________________

PRIORITIES

☐ ____________________
☐ ____________________
☐ ____________________
☐ ____________________
☐ ____________________
☐ ____________________
☐ ____________________

NOTES

REMINDER

Notes

Chapter 7 – Becoming a Master Manifestor

We want you to know that, this is a deep and sacred chapter because here we're not just teaching how to manifest money, but how to become a Master Manifestor — someone who commands reality with clarity, vibration, and precision.

Here, you are also given so much richness to work with (language, subconscious programming, energy, vibration), so we'll expand further in this Chapter (7).

Chapter 7 — Becoming a Master Manifestor
Manipulating Energy the Right Way

Energy is obedient. It does not question you, it does not argue, it does not negotiate. Energy simply follows your command. The question is: are you commanding it with clarity, or are you scattering it with confusion?

To manipulate energy the right way, you must:

- Set clear intentions — know exactly what you are calling in.
- Release resistance — no doubt, no "what if," no double talk.
- Command with awareness — speak consciously, not casually.
- Hold consistency — your words, your feelings, and your actions must match.

When intention, vibration, and action align, energy has no choice but to obey.

When intention, vibration, and action align, energy has no choice but to obey.

Training the Subconscious to See Wealth as Normal

The subconscious is the master program that runs your life. It does not care about your dreams; it only obeys repetition and belief. If you constantly speak of struggle, lack, and doubt, your subconscious will make those your reality. If you constantly affirm wealth, overflow, and victory, your subconscious will normalize abundance.

To train your subconscious:

- Repeat affirmations daily with feeling.
- Visualize wealth until it feels ordinary.
- Surround yourself with reminders of abundance.
- Eliminate negative jokes, self-sabotage, and careless words.

The subconscious is like soil—it grows whatever you plant.

The "Already Done" Mindset

Master Manifestors never say, "One day I will…" They say, "It is already done." This mindset bends time, collapses resistance, and places you in the reality of already having.

- Not "I will win," but "I have won."
- Not "I will be rich," but "I am rich."
- Not "I will be healed," but "I am healed."

The universe mirrors certainty. The more you live as if it's already done, the faster it manifests into form.

Seeing It, Feeling It, Believing It — Then Receiving It

Manifestation is a full-body practice. You cannot just think abundance—you must feel it, believe it, and live it.

1. See it — visualize your win, your health, your love, your legacy.
2. Feel it — let your body experience the emotions of having it now.
3. Believe it — speak it with no doubt, no second-guessing.
4. Receive it — act as if it is already here, and watch it unfold.

The Power of Language

Words are spells. They are vibrations that instruct your cells and your reality. The universe does not ask if you are joking, careless, or exaggerating. It obeys. That is why self-deprecating jokes, negative phrases, or chaotic language shape chaotic outcomes.

English is full of traps:

- "Spend" when you mean "invest."
- "Work hard" when you mean "create with ease."
- "Wake" when you mean "rise."
- "Deadline" when you mean "lifeline."

Your cells hear and obey every word, whether you know it or not.

This is why high-vibrational languages like Kreyòl (Haitian Creole, or Kraol, there have been so many discoveries about this lately, another conversation for another day) hold so much power. In Kreyòl, what is spoken is what is understood—direct, clear, and vibrationally aligned. Kreyòl pale, Kreyòl konprann — Creole is spoken, Creole is understood. No confusion, no distortion.

Do yourself a favor: learn and use languages that uplift, clarify, and align. Speak with precision. Choose words that carry light, not lack.

Dare to Change Your Mind

Becoming a Master Manifestor means daring to change the very way you think, speak, and feel. Too many times, we speak against ourselves effortlessly—but struggle to speak for ourselves with the same power. That must end.

- Do not curse yourself in humor.
- Do not repeat words that bind you in lack.
- Do not agree with energies that lower your vibration.

Your cells obey. The universe obeys. They never ask, "*Did you mean that*?" They simply follow your command. So let your command always be life, abundance, and victory.

Affirmations for Master Manifestors

1. I speak with clarity, and the universe obeys me.
2. My cells hear my words and align with health, wealth, and abundance.
3. I eliminate confusion; my language is precise, powerful, and high-frequency.
4. I see it, I feel it, I believe it, and I receive it now.
5. My subconscious is trained to expect and normalize wealth.
6. I command energy with awareness, and energy answers me.
7. It is already done—I live as a master manifestor.

Declaration of Mastery

"I no longer scatter my energy. I command it. I no longer beg reality to change—I change my reality with words, vibration, and belief. My subconscious is trained to welcome wealth, my cells obey my affirmations, my language is precise and powerful. I see it, I feel it, I believe it, I receive it. It is already done. I am a Master Manifestor."

The Discipline of Speech

Every word is a command, and every command has a consequence. This is why ancient traditions taught people to speak less, to guard their tongue, and to measure their words with wisdom.

- Sometimes it is better to stay silent than to run your mouth.
- Sometimes readiness is not in speaking more, but in resisting less.
- True mastery is harmony: your mind, your words, and your environment moving as one.

If the environment you are in depletes you, change it. If your words are draining you, stop them. If your tongue is writing commands that sabotage you, quiet it.

Even in casual moments—venting, chatting, joking—be aware. The universe and your cells are always listening. What you slightly "let slip" still programs your reality.

Now that you know better, do better. Speak with awareness. Write with intention. Share with discernment. Silence is also a frequency, and sometimes it is the highest one.

TO DO LIST

DATE: ____________ DUE DATE ____________

TO DO

☐ ____________
☐ ____________
☐ ____________
☐ ____________
☐ ____________
☐ ____________
☐ ____________
☐ ____________
☐ ____________
☐ ____________
☐ ____________
☐ ____________
☐ ____________
☐ ____________
☐ ____________
☐ ____________
☐ ____________
☐ ____________
☐ ____________
☐ ____________
☐ ____________
☐ ____________
☐ ____________
☐ ____________
☐ ____________
☐ ____________

PRIORITIES

☐ ____________
☐ ____________
☐ ____________
☐ ____________
☐ ____________
☐ ____________
☐ ____________

NOTES

REMINDER

Notes

Chapter 7 – REPEAT Becoming a Master Manifestor

Author's Note on Repetition

As you read this book, you may notice that some ideas – especially in Chapter 7 and in other key places – appear more than once. This is not by accident. Repetition is one of the most powerful tools to reprogram the subconscious mind.

When you hear something once, it may inspire you. When you hear it again, it begins to take root. And when you repeat it enough times, it becomes a part of you – an unshakable truth.

So yes, certain affirmations, practices, and warnings are repeated in these pages. They are imperative. They are meant to reach deeper into you until your cells, your spirit, and your subconscious all respond with, "I know this. I live this. This is who I am."

Do not skip over repetition. Embrace it. Every time you meet it again, let it sink further into your mind and spirit. Because sometimes, hearing it the second or third time is when it finally becomes real for you.

Manipulating Energy the Right Way

Energy is obedient. It does not question you, it does not argue, it does not negotiate. Energy simply follows your command. The question is: are you commanding it with clarity, or scattering it with confusion?

To manipulate energy the right way, you must:

- Set clear intentions — know exactly what you are calling in.
- Release resistance — no doubt, no "what if," no double talk.
- Command with awareness — speak consciously, not casually.
- Hold consistency — your words, your feelings, and your actions must match.

When intention, vibration, and action align, energy has no choice but to obey.

Training the Subconscious to See Wealth as Normal

The subconscious is the master program that runs your life. It does not care about your dreams; it only obeys repetition and belief.

- If you constantly speak of struggle, lack, and doubt, your subconscious will make those your reality.

- If you constantly affirm wealth, overflow, and victory, your subconscious will normalize abundance.

To train your subconscious:

- Repeat affirmations daily with emotion.
- Visualize wealth until it feels ordinary.
- Surround yourself with reminders of abundance.
- Eliminate negative jokes, careless words, and self-sabotage.

The subconscious is like soil—it grows whatever you plant.

The "Already Done" Mindset

Master Manifestors never say, "One day I will…"
They say, "It is already done."

- Not "I will win," but "I have won."
- Not "I will be rich," but "I am rich."
- Not "I will be healed," but "I am healed."

The universe mirrors certainty. The more you live as if it's already done, the faster it manifests into form.

Seeing It, Feeling It, Believing It — Then Receiving It

Manifestation is not a single thought—it is a whole-body practice.

1. See it — visualize your win, your health, your love, your legacy.
2. Feel it — let your body experience the emotions of having it now.
3. Believe it — speak it with no doubt or hesitation.
4. Receive it — act as if it is already here, and watch it unfold.

The Power of Language

Words are spells. They are vibrations that instruct your cells and your reality. The universe does not ask if you are joking, careless, or exaggerating—it simply obeys.

English is full of traps:

- "Spend" when you mean "invest."
- "Work hard" when you mean "create with ease."
- "Wake" when you mean "rise."
- "Deadline" when you mean "lifeline."

Your cells hear and obey every word, whether you know it or not.

This is why high-vibrational languages like Kreyòl (Haitian Creole, Kraol) carry such power. In Kreyòl, what is spoken is what is understood—direct, clear, and aligned. Kreyòl pale, Kreyòl konprann — Creole is spoken, Creole is understood. No confusion, no distortion.

Do yourself a favor: learn and use languages that uplift, clarify, and align. Speak with precision. Choose words that carry light, not lack.

The Discipline of Speech

Every word is a command, and every command has a consequence. This is why ancient traditions taught people to speak less, to guard their tongue, and to measure their words carefully.

- Sometimes it is better to stay silent than to run your mouth.
- Sometimes readiness is not in speaking more, but in resisting less.
- True mastery is harmony: your mind, your words, and your environment moving as one.

If your environment is depleting you, leave it. If your words are draining you, stop them. If your tongue is writing commands that sabotage you, quiet it.

Even in casual moments—venting, chatting, joking—be aware. The universe and your cells are always listening. What you "let slip" still programs your reality.

Now that you know better, do better. Speak with awareness. Write with intention. Share with discernment. Silence is also a frequency, and sometimes it is the highest one.

Affirmations for Master Manifestors

1. I speak with clarity, and the universe obeys me.
2. My cells hear my words and align with health, wealth, and abundance.
3. I eliminate confusion; my language is precise, powerful, and high-frequency.
4. I see it, I feel it, I believe it, and I receive it now.
5. My subconscious is trained to expect and normalize wealth.
6. I command energy with awareness, and energy answers me.
7. It is already done—I live as a Master Manifestor.

Declaration of Mastery

"I no longer scatter my energy—I command it.
I no longer beg reality to change—I change reality with my words, vibration, and belief.
My subconscious is trained to welcome wealth.
My cells obey my affirmations.
My language is precise, clear, and high-frequency.
I see it, I feel it, I believe it, I receive it.
It is already done. I am a Master Manifestor."

Chapter 7 is for you, it is — a balance of teaching, warnings, language mastery, affirmations, and a strong declaration.
Then, moving into Chapter 8, it is about — Honoring Ancestors & Crossing Over, where we anchor wealth with gratitude, libations, and ancestral alignment.

TO DO LIST

DATE: ____________ DUE DATE ____________

TO DO

- [ ] ____________
- [ ] ____________
- [ ] ____________
- [ ] ____________
- [ ] ____________
- [ ] ____________
- [ ] ____________
- [ ] ____________
- [ ] ____________
- [ ] ____________
- [ ] ____________
- [ ] ____________
- [ ] ____________
- [ ] ____________
- [ ] ____________
- [ ] ____________
- [ ] ____________
- [ ] ____________
- [ ] ____________
- [ ] ____________
- [ ] ____________
- [ ] ____________
- [ ] ____________
- [ ] ____________
- [ ] ____________
- [ ] ____________

PRIORITIES

- [ ] ____________
- [ ] ____________
- [ ] ____________
- [ ] ____________
- [ ] ____________
- [ ] ____________
- [ ] ____________

NOTES

REMINDER

Notes

Chapter 8 – Honoring Ancestors & Crossing Over

How Ancestors Align You with Abundance

You are not standing alone. You are the result of every step, every sacrifice, every prayer, and every breath of those who came before you. When wealth arrives, it is not only your win—it is theirs too. Ancestors often align doors, numbers, and opportunities so that blessings reach the ones who carry their blood.

When you honor them, you strengthen the flow. When you ignore them, the blessing may feel heavy, empty, or easily wasted. Abundance flows most freely when it is connected to lineage.

Libations, Gratitude, and Remembrance After a Win

When the jackpot is in your hands, remember gratitude before spending.

- Pour libations of water, rum, coffee, or flowers to the earth. Speak the names of your ancestors. Thank them for clearing the path.
- Light a candle, play their favorite song, or cook their favorite meal in their honor.
- Keep a journal of gratitude, writing down how they shaped your strength.

Gratitude anchors wealth. It transforms it from a mere number into a sacred inheritance.

Gratitude anchors wealth. It transforms it from a mere number into a sacred inheritance.

Making Your Wealth Sacred, Not Wasted

Money in careless hands becomes poison. Money in sacred hands becomes medicine.

Sacred wealth means:

- Investing (Spending) with intention, not impulse.
- Investing in what heals, builds, and uplifts.
- Creating legacies that restore your family line.
- Treating money as a spiritual tool, not just a material one.

Waste is what happens when you forget purpose. Sacred use is what happens when you remember you are part of something greater than yourself.

Why Honoring the Past Protects Your Future

When you honor the past, you secure the future. Ancestors who are remembered stand as guardians; they shield you from betrayal, confusion, and sabotage. They whisper wisdom in dreams, send you warnings, and clear blockages that wealth alone cannot.

By remembering them, you do two things:

- You acknowledge that you did not win alone.
- You secure their guidance to protect the blessings ahead.

Forget them, and the future becomes shaky. Honor them, and the future is fortified.

Affirmations for Ancestral Alignment

- I honor those who walked before me; they walk with me still.
- My ancestors align me with abundance and guard my path.
- I make my wealth sacred, not wasted.
- Gratitude flows from me as freely as abundance flows to me.
- I am a vessel for my lineage, a guardian of legacy.
- I am protected by the wisdom of the past and guided into the future.
- My wealth is my offering, my gratitude, and my testimony.

Declaration of Ancestral Wealth

"This win is not mine alone
—it belongs to my bloodline.
I honor the prayers of my ancestors.
I give thanks to the sacrifices
that cleared my path.
I pour libations,
I lift gratitude,
I sanctify my abundance.
My wealth is sacred,
my wealth is protected,
my wealth is eternal.
By honoring the past, I secure the future.
I walk with them, they walk with me.
Together, we are victorious."

Chapter 8 now closes the practical with the spiritual, grounding abundance in ancestral reverence.

Chapter 9: The Conclusion — The True Jackpot. This is where we tie the entire journey together and remind you that the biggest win is not just money, but alignment, clarity, and purpose.

May this book be truly what you've been looking for and what you've manifested in your life. May it be that good luck charm you've been looking for.

TO DO LIST

DATE: ______________________ DUE DATE ______________________

TO DO

- [ ] ______________________
- [ ] ______________________
- [ ] ______________________
- [ ] ______________________
- [ ] ______________________
- [ ] ______________________
- [ ] ______________________
- [ ] ______________________
- [ ] ______________________
- [ ] ______________________
- [ ] ______________________
- [ ] ______________________
- [ ] ______________________
- [ ] ______________________
- [ ] ______________________
- [ ] ______________________
- [ ] ______________________
- [ ] ______________________
- [ ] ______________________
- [ ] ______________________
- [ ] ______________________
- [ ] ______________________
- [ ] ______________________
- [ ] ______________________
- [ ] ______________________
- [ ] ______________________

PRIORITIES

- [ ] ______________________
- [ ] ______________________
- [ ] ______________________
- [ ] ______________________
- [ ] ______________________
- [ ] ______________________
- [ ] ______________________

NOTES

REMINDER

Notes

Chapter 9 – The Conclusion: The True Jackpot

Chapter 9 — The Conclusion: The True Jackpot

The Real Win

The jackpot is not only in the ticket. The true jackpot is in the mind that dares to align, the tongue that speaks life, the spirit that honors its ancestors, and the heart that moves with clarity and gratitude. Money may multiply, but without wisdom it vanishes. Wisdom, alignment, and purpose—that is the treasure no one can take away.

You Are Already the Winner

The greatest shift you can ever make is to understand that you are already the winner. Before the numbers are called, before the ticket is drawn, before the bank account grows—you are the jackpot. You are abundance walking, prosperity breathing, legacy alive.

The wealth outside is only a reflection of the wealth within. When you keep your mind disciplined, your words precise, your spirit grateful, and your actions aligned, you can never lose.

Living as a Winner Daily

- Guard your energy.
- Speak only words that create life.
- Align with gratitude every morning.
- Honor your ancestors.
- Protect your peace.
- Invest in yourself and your legacy.

Every day lived with these practices is a winning day, with or without a lottery ticket.

Affirmations of the True Jackpot

1. I am the jackpot.
2. I am the wealth, the blessing, the abundance.
3. My spirit is rich, and my life reflects it.
4. I am grateful for the past, present, and future.
5. My words create, my actions multiply, my legacy lives.
6. I win daily because I am aligned daily.
7. I am the true treasure, and I overflow.

Final Declaration

"I am the jackpot, the abundance, the legacy.
I am the blessing that multiplies blessings.
Money is my tool, not my master.
Wealth flows through me, not just to me.
I honor my ancestors, I protect my peace,
I secure my future.
I was born to win, and I remain a winner.
The true jackpot is me."

Reminders — Quick Aha Moments & Things to Take With You

- Play responsibly — never gamble what you can't afford to lose.
- Breathe and align — energy follows calm certainty, not desperation.
- Words are spells — every word you speak commands your reality.

- Say "I have," not "I need" — the vibration of ownership draws wealth.
- Prepare your Winner's List now — don't wait until the jackpot arrives.
- First 72 hours matter — stay quiet, stay safe, ground yourself.

- Protect yourself unapologetically — your safety comes before sharing.
- Upgrade your mindset — poverty thinking drains, millionaire thinking multiplies.
- Invest wisely — property, business, self, and legacy.

- Don't forget health, love, and joy — money supports but cannot replace them.
- Honor your ancestors — gratitude keeps wealth sacred and protected.
- Silence is powerful — sometimes saying less aligns you more.
- You are already the jackpot — money is only the reflection of who you are inside.

The Winner's Prayer

"Creator of all abundance,
I give thanks for the blessings already placed in my life.

I thank You for wisdom greater than wealth,
for peace deeper than riches,
for joy stronger than fear.

I thank You for the ancestors who walked before me,
whose prayers and sacrifices opened this door.

I ask that You guide my hands
to use my wealth wisely,
to protect my safety,
to honor my lineage,
and to bless others without losing myself.

May my winnings never be wasted.
May my abundance never be corrupted.

May my heart remain humble,
my mind remain clear,
and my spirit remain aligned with truth.

I am the jackpot.
I am the blessing.
I am the legacy.

So it is, and so it will forever be."

Winner's Protection Prayer

"Divine Source of all power,
I stand as Your Chosen Vessel of Abundance.
Protect me from every plot, every trap,
every weapon formed against me.
Let no scheme prosper, let no tongue undo me,
let no energy defeat me.

If enemies rise against me,
let them fall asleep and forget me.
If they plan against me,
let the plan scatter before it reaches me.
If I am ever about to stumble,
rearrange the universe in my favor.
Turn every danger into my deliverance,
every attack into my advancement.

Keep me hidden when I must be hidden,
and visible only in ways that bring honor and blessing.
Place me always in the right environment,
surrounded by allies, even if they once came as enemies.
Transform their hands to serve and protect me,
whether they know it or not.

Shield my mind from the world's programming,
from fear, greed, and distraction.
Anchor me in truth, awareness, and divine clarity.
I walk with wisdom, I speak with power,
I move with certainty.
For I am the jackpot, the abundance, the chosen.

No weapon formed against me shall prosper.

Every step I take is secured,
every breath I breathe is blessed,
and everything works for my good.

So it is, so it must be, and so it already is."

Closing Blessings

The Winner's Prayer of Gratitude

"Creator of all abundance,
I give thanks for the blessings already placed in my life.
I thank You for wisdom greater than wealth,
for peace deeper than riches,
for joy stronger than fear.

I thank You for the ancestors who walked before me,
whose prayers and sacrifices opened this door.

I ask that You guide my hands
to use my wealth wisely,
to protect my safety,
to honor my lineage,
and to bless others without losing myself.

May my winnings never be wasted.
May my abundance never be corrupted.
May my heart remain humble, my mind remain clear,
and my spirit remain aligned with truth.

I am the jackpot.
I am the blessing.
I am the legacy.

So it is, and so it will forever be."

The Winner's Protection Prayer (again)

"Divine Source of all power,
I stand as Your chosen vessel of abundance.
Protect me from every plot, every trap,
every weapon formed against me.
Let no scheme prosper,
let no tongue undo me,
let no energy defeat me.

If enemies rise against me,
let them fall asleep and forget me.
If they plan against me,
let the plan scatter before it reaches me.
If I am ever about to stumble,
rearrange the universe in my favor.
Turn every danger into my deliverance,
every attack into my advancement.

Keep me hidden when I must be hidden,
and visible only in ways that bring honor and blessing.
Place me always in the right environment,
surrounded by allies, even if they once came as enemies.
Transform their hands to serve and protect me,
whether they know it or not.

Shield my mind from the world's programming,
from fear, greed, and distraction.
Anchor me in truth, awareness, and divine clarity.

I walk with wisdom,

I speak with power,
I move with certainty.

I walk with wisdom,
I speak with power,
I move with certainty.
For I am the jackpot,
the abundance, the chosen.

No weapon formed against me shall prosper.

Every step I take is secured,
every breath I breathe is blessed,
and everything works for my good.

So it is, so it must be, and so it already is."

Conclusion — The True Jackpot

Wealth in Spirit, Health, and Love

The numbers, the ticket, the millions — these are symbols, not the source. True wealth is in your spirit, your health, and your love. Money without peace is misery. Riches without health are fragile. Success without love is empty. But when wealth supports these deeper treasures, you are complete.

Gratitude and Alignment Every Day

Abundance is not a one-time event. It is a daily practice. Every sunrise is an opportunity to realign. Gratitude is the magnet that keeps blessings flowing. When you live each day with thankfulness, you lock yourself into the frequency of receiving more.

You Are Already the Winner

Whether or not the ticket falls into your hand, you are already the jackpot. The fact that you breathe, dream, love, and walk with spirit means you are living abundance. The external win is just the reflection of the internal truth: you are the blessing, the prize, the legacy.

You are not waiting for fortune — you are fortune. You are not chasing millions — millions chase you. You are not trying to win — you are already the winner.

Affirmations of the True Jackpot

1. I am wealthy in spirit, health, and love.
2. Gratitude aligns me with endless blessings.
3. I win daily, no matter the numbers.
4. My abundance is permanent, within and without.
5. I am already the jackpot.

Final Declaration

"I am the true jackpot.
I am wealth in spirit,
health, love, and legacy.
Money is my servant,
not my master.

Gratitude is my daily practice,
alignment is my way of life.

I was born to win, I live to win,
and I remain a winner.

I am the blessing,
I am the prize,
I am the abundance.

So it is, and so it will forever be."

TO DO LIST

DATE: ____________________ DUE DATE ____________________

TO DO

- [ ] ____________________
- [ ] ____________________
- [ ] ____________________
- [ ] ____________________
- [ ] ____________________
- [ ] ____________________
- [ ] ____________________
- [ ] ____________________
- [ ] ____________________
- [ ] ____________________
- [ ] ____________________
- [ ] ____________________
- [ ] ____________________
- [ ] ____________________
- [ ] ____________________
- [ ] ____________________
- [ ] ____________________
- [ ] ____________________
- [ ] ____________________
- [ ] ____________________
- [ ] ____________________
- [ ] ____________________
- [ ] ____________________
- [ ] ____________________
- [ ] ____________________
- [ ] ____________________

PRIORITIES

- [ ] ____________________
- [ ] ____________________
- [ ] ____________________
- [ ] ____________________
- [ ] ____________________
- [ ] ____________________
- [ ] ____________________

NOTES

REMINDER

Notes

BONUS:

Exercises for Winners — Mindset, Self-Upgrade, and Possibility

1. The Mirror Declaration

- Stand in front of a mirror morning and night.
- Look into your own eyes and say out loud:
- "I am the jackpot. I am already the winner. My abundance is certain, my millions are mine."
- Repeat 7 times until your voice grows steady and strong.

2. The Winner's Journal

Every night, write in a dedicated notebook:

- Three things you are grateful for today.
- One affirmation in "I have" language (e.g., "I have financial freedom").
- A short vision of what you will do with your win (just one detail each night—house, charity, vacation, etc.).
- This conditions the subconscious to normalize wealth.

3. The Visualization Upgrade

- Close your eyes, take 3 deep breaths.
- Visualize your jackpot check, account balance, or ticket.
- Now add detail: what you're wearing, who's with you, how you're smiling, where you're standing.
- Stay in that vision until your body feels joy as if it already happened.

4. Language Detox

For one week, track your words. Anytime you say:

- "I need," "I want," "I can't," or self-deprecating jokes—
- catch yourself and reframe into "I have," "I am," "I will," "I can."
- Write down examples daily. By the end of the week, you'll see your upgrade in clarity.

5. The Ancestor Gratitude Practice

- Light a candle or pour a libation of water.
- Speak out loud: "I honor you for aligning me with abundance."
- Share your dreams with them: "I will use my winnings to build, to bless, to heal."
- Close with: "Walk with me as I walk in overflow."

6. The Environment Check

Ask yourself:

- Does this place/relationship/job drain me or align me?
- If it drains, write one action to shift it (leave, change habits, set boundaries).
- If it aligns, write how you will nourish it further.
- Abundance thrives in the right environment.

7. The Jackpot Patience Practice

Sit in silence for 5 minutes daily and repeat slowly:

"Under grace, in perfect time, my jackpot is certain. I am already the winner."

Let your body relax into patience. This dissolves desperation and strengthens trust.

The Winner's Practice: Daily Exercises to Align With Abundance

A sacred set of actions to shift your mindset, upgrade your self, and accept the endless possibilities that wealth and alignment are already yours.

1. The Mirror Declaration
Stand in front of a mirror, look yourself in the eye, and repeat 7 times:
"I am the jackpot. My abundance is already here."

2. The Winner's Journal
Each night write:

- 3 gratitudes
- 1 "I have" affirmation
- 1 vision detail of what you'll do with your win

3. Visualization Upgrade
Close your eyes, breathe deeply, and see yourself holding the win. Add sensory details until your body feels joy.

4. Language Detox
Track your words for one week. Anytime you say "I need" or "I can't", reframe instantly to "I have" or "I can."

5. Ancestor Gratitude Practice
Light a candle or pour water and say:
"I honor you for aligning me with abundance." Share your dreams aloud.

6. Environment Check

Write down who and what drains you vs. what aligns you. Take one action to shift into the right environment.

7. Jackpot Patience Practice

Sit in silence daily and whisper:

"Under grace, in perfect time, my jackpot is certain."

Reminders — Quick Aha Moments & Things to Take With You

A short cheat sheet of key truths (responsible play, language, alignment, protection, gratitude, ancestors, etc.).

Closing Blessings

The Winner's Prayer of Gratitude

- Thanking Creator and ancestors for abundance, wisdom, and legacy.
- Sealing wealth with humility and joy.

The Winner's Protection Prayer

- Shielding from betrayal, plots, and distractions.
- Securing safety, clarity, and divine favor.

The Winner's Practice: Daily Exercises to Align With Abundance

1. Mirror Declaration (daily affirmations face-to-face).
2. Winner's Journal (gratitude + "I have" statements).
3. Visualization Upgrade (see, feel, believe, receive).
4. Language Detox (reframe lack into abundance).
5. Ancestor Gratitude Practice (libations, offerings, remembrance).
6. Environment Check (remove drains, strengthen alignments).
7. Jackpot Patience Practice (silence, grace, and trust).

With this flow, you find:

- Reminders (quick clarity),
- Blessings (spiritual sealing),
- Exercises (practical application).

It's like mind, spirit, and body all aligned to leave you truly equipped.

TO DO LIST

DATE: ____________________ DUE DATE ____________________

TO DO

- ☐ ____________________
- ☐ ____________________
- ☐ ____________________
- ☐ ____________________
- ☐ ____________________
- ☐ ____________________
- ☐ ____________________
- ☐ ____________________
- ☐ ____________________
- ☐ ____________________
- ☐ ____________________
- ☐ ____________________
- ☐ ____________________
- ☐ ____________________
- ☐ ____________________
- ☐ ____________________
- ☐ ____________________
- ☐ ____________________
- ☐ ____________________
- ☐ ____________________
- ☐ ____________________
- ☐ ____________________
- ☐ ____________________
- ☐ ____________________
- ☐ ____________________
- ☐ ____________________

PRIORITIES

- ☐ ____________________
- ☐ ____________________
- ☐ ____________________
- ☐ ____________________
- ☐ ____________________
- ☐ ____________________
- ☐ ____________________

NOTES

REMINDER

Notes

Bonus Chapter — Beware of False Numbers & False Gifts

The Online Trap

Every day, on social media and in private messages, people claim they have the winning numbers for the lottery. Some ask for money in exchange for the "secret." Others pretend they are spiritually gifted, chosen to give you the numbers. Many are scammers, and others are energy harvesters who trade in forces you cannot see.

If they truly had the power to call numbers at will, why would they need you to play? Why would they not share with their own family and friends? Why would they charge strangers instead of walking quietly into abundance themselves?

The truth: when it is your time, it is your time. No one can manipulate destiny that belongs to you.

Spiritual Risks of False Numbers

What many do not realize is that sometimes these numbers are not "gifts" but traps. They may come from dark spiritual dealings. When you play numbers given by someone tied to such forces, you are unknowingly entering their ritual.

- You may be volunteering your energy, your bloodline, or your protection.

- You may be placing yourself under agreements you did not consciously make.
- You may be sacrificing your alignment by allowing them access to your life.

Do not give your power away so easily.

A Better Path: Fasting & Discipline

True winning comes not from shortcuts, but from alignment.

- Fast to cleanse your body and spirit.
- Discipline your words, your mindset, your focus, and your habits. Train your language.
- Align your vibration with abundance through affirmations, gratitude, and protection. So repeat affirmations, live in gratitude, protect your energy.

This is the safe, sacred way to abundance. Shortcuts offered by strangers often lead to danger, debt, or spiritual entanglement. Whilst these practices build the kind of vessel wealth can safely rest in.

Protect Yourself Always

Whenever someone offers you anything—numbers, advice, opportunities—stop and ask:

- Where is this coming from?
- What do they want in return?
- Is this aligned with divine order, or is it manipulation?

Protect yourself with prayer, discernment, and intuition. Do not let curiosity or desperation pull you into rituals you never meant to join.

Affirmations of Discernment

1. I have discernment and clarity; no scam can deceive me.
2. I trust divine timing; my win is secured in grace.
3. I am protected from energy harvesters and false gifts.
4. I play aligned, disciplined, and fearless.
5. I guard my power, and I never give it away.
6. My abundance flows through alignment, not shortcuts.

Declaration of Protection from False Numbers

"I do not fall for false gifts. I do not chase what is not mine. I do not volunteer myself into hidden rituals. I trust divine timing and divine alignment. My jackpot arrives under grace, with clarity and safety. No stranger holds my destiny. No scammer holds my fortune. My power is my own, and I protect it fiercely. So it is, and so it will always be."

This Bonus Chapter is to close the book — a sacred warning that balances the teachings of faith and manifestation with spiritual discernment and protection. This Bonus Chapter now closes with both a warning and a reassurance: scams can't touch you, and when it's truly your time, the universe will make sure you know.

We are sharing this with you because that's exactly the other side of discernment — knowing when the numbers come from alignment, not manipulation. We want you to know that this is your time, your moment, and your opportunity to grasp this truth and make something out of it, and if it is truly your divine time, the universe will make it unmistakable.

When It Is Truly Your Time

If numbers are meant for you, they will not come through manipulation or strangers seeking payment. They will arrive through alignment, intuition, and divine timing.

- You may dream the numbers, or see them repeated in ways that feel undeniable.
- You may receive a gentle nudge from your spirit or your ancestors — a hint, a whisper, a vision.
- You may notice the numbers are tied to meaningful dates: birthdays, anniversaries, sacred times.
- A loved one who has crossed over may appear in your dream with guidance, as if blessing your path.
- Even when you hesitate, the universe may arrange circumstances so that you must step out, and the act of playing aligns perfectly.

When it is truly your time, the experience will feel natural, safe, and guided. You will feel peace, not desperation. You will feel clarity, not confusion.

Your gut will always tell you the difference. If your spirit feels unsettled, stop immediately. Do not force, do not bargain, do not second-guess. True abundance never requires you to sacrifice your safety, your soul, or your peace.

When it is your jackpot moment, you will know.

Know that this Bonus Chapter is all about discernment and protecting your energy, we created this vow which aligns with its message and title. This is a Vow of Discernment & Divine Timing, reinforcing that no one else holds your jackpot but you.

The Vow: Beware of False Numbers & False Gifts

"I vow to never give my power away.
I vow to trust divine timing,
knowing my win arrives under grace and in perfect order.

I vow to honor my gut, my spirit,
and my intuition — for they always tell me the truth.
I vow to never chase shortcuts, nor follow
false gifts that drain my soul.

I vow to protect my lineage, my energy, and my destiny.
I vow to stay aligned with clarity, discipline, and discernment.
When it is my time, I will know, and
I will walk into it with peace, certainty, and joy.

No scammer holds my jackpot.
No stranger holds my fortune.
No force can take what is already mine.

I am aligned, I am protected, I am patient, I am certain.
My abundance arrives pure, safe, and divinely sealed.
So it is, so it must be, and so it already is."

Quick Mantra of Discernment

"No one holds my jackpot but me. My win is safe in divine timing."

This is: Simple, powerful, and easy to repeat under the breath like armor.

7 Mantras of Discernment & Protection

1. I trust divine timing; my win is mine alone.
2. No scammer, no stranger, no spirit holds my destiny.
3. I guard my energy and never give it away.
4. When it is my time, I will know with clarity and peace.
5. I am protected from false numbers and false gifts.
6. My jackpot comes under grace, not through shortcuts.
7. I am sealed, safe, and aligned with true abundance.

7 Declarations of Discernment & Protection

1. I declare that no scammer, stranger, or manipulator will ever deceive me, for I walk in clarity and divine truth.
2. I declare that my energy is sealed, my lineage is guarded, and no false gift can enter my life.
3. I declare that I am patient, disciplined, and aligned with perfect timing — I do not chase shortcuts.
4. I declare that any plot, trap, or hidden treatment (ritual)formed against me scatters before it reaches me.
5. I declare that when my jackpot comes, it will come safely, purely, and without strings attached.
6. I declare that my intuition speaks loudly, my discernment guides me, and my spirit cannot be tricked.
7. I declare that I am protected under grace, aligned in truth, and my abundance is eternal.

Know that each Bonus Chapter is as a shield and safeguard and the prayer below closes the bonus chapters.

Prayer of Protection from False Numbers & False Gifts

"Divine Source of Light and Truth,
I stand in Your clarity and protection.
No scammer can deceive me,
no harvester can drain me,
no stranger can trick me into giving away my destiny.

Shield my mind from confusion,
my heart from desperation,
and my spirit from hidden rituals.
If I am tempted, awaken my discernment.
If I am pressured, strengthen my no.
If I am tested, let truth and peace guide me back to alignment.

Let every false gift scatter before it reaches me.
Let every trap collapse before I step into it.
Let every plot turn to dust in the presence of my light.

I am sealed in divine timing,
I am aligned with pure abundance,
I am protected by grace.

My jackpot comes only from truth,
and nothing unclean will ever touch it.

So it is, and so it will always be."

Closing Letter to the Reader

Beloved Winner,
If you are holding this book in your hands, know this: the universe already calls you chosen. You did not arrive here by accident. Every page you read was a reminder of who you already are — the jackpot, the abundance, the blessing.

May you never again wait for permission to shine.
May you never again give your power away to strangers, fear, or desperation. May you rise daily with gratitude, with clarity, with protection.

Be patient with yourself, and trust the timing of your life. When it is your moment, nothing and no one can block you. Until then, live as if it is already done — because in truth, it is.

Remember: wealth is not only in numbers. It is in your spirit, your health, your love, your legacy. Walk richly, speak richly, live richly. Protect your peace fiercely, and honor those who came before you.

I leave you with this truth: You are not chasing millions. Millions are chasing you. You are not trying to win. You are the win. You are the jackpot.
So it is, and so it will forever be.

With strength, clarity, and love,
Rev. Dr. Marie Brevil

Note to SELF or place a picture before you won.

Note to SELF or place a picture when you found out you won.

Note to SELF or place a picture of you after you know that you won.

Notes

Notes

Notes

Made in the USA
Monee, IL
04 November 2026

67377574R00098